OLYSLAGER AUTO LIBRARY

Fairground and Circus Transport

compiled by the OLYSLAGER ORGANISATION

research by Denis N. Miller

edited by Bart H. Vanderveen

FREDERICK WARNE & Co Ltd
London and New York

THE OLYSLAGER AUTO LIBRARY

This book is one of a growing range of titles on major transport subjects.
Titles published so far include:

The Jeep
Half-Tracks
Scammell Vehicles
Fire-Fighting Vehicles
Earth-Moving Vehicles
Wreckers and Recovery Vehicles
Passenger Vehicles
Fairground and Circus Transport

American Cars of the 1930s
American Cars of the 1940s
American Cars of the 1950s

British Cars of the Early Thirties
British Cars of the Late Thirties

Library of Congress Catalog Card No. 73-80249

ISBN 0 7232 1727 0

Filmset and printed in Great Britain
by BAS Printers Limited, Wallop, Hampshire

461-473

Without a reliable means of transport, the modern travelling showman's business is doomed to failure. Whilst remaining totally economical, his vehicles must serve as load-carriers, mobile homes and generating plants and he must be a 'jack-of-all-trades', capable of repairing any equipment which may break down or damage which may be caused, and even building his own rides or adapting existing machines.

Before 1860 practically all transport was horse-drawn and riding machines as we know them were unheard of. The fairground would consist largely of one-man or family concerns, each outfit comprising perhaps one or two wagons normally hauled by no more than two horses each. Occasionally, however, one could see trains of three or more large wagons hauled by a number of horses, and the larger travelling menageries, operating mainly independently of the fairgrounds, often had as many as 50 or 60 horses hauling some fourteen heavy loads (e.g. Wombwell's first show of the 1880s).

Although a handful of tenting circuses continued to use equine transport as late as the 1920s and Thirties, it is claimed that the first application of self-propulsion in this field was by the American circus proprietor Jim Myer who, as early as 1859, while on a tour of Southern England, purchased a Bray traction engine which he decorated with carved wood and bright paintwork, setting a precedent in showland decoration carried on to this day.

There are showmen, notably in the United States and Canada, who rely upon the railway system to move their equipment from town to town, many fair and circus grounds being located conveniently alongside freight sidings. In the British Isles, however, the relatively short distances travelled combined with a basically inadequate railway system have led to the showman's reliance upon vehicular movement. It was the British showman, therefore, who was largely responsible for the introduction of the road train, sometimes consisting of seven or more wagons, hauled by a gleaming example of the showman's steam road locomotive or scenic engine, both familiar products of British heavy industry.

These immense road trains became illegal during the Thirties and now only three trailers can be hauled at any one time by a 'heavy locomotive', provided that the total combination does not exceed a given length.

In the United Kingdom, the home of the travelling showman, his interests are well represented in Parliament by the Showman's Guild. Any legislation which may affect his activities is closely studied by the Guild and this usually results in some form of exemption. There are, for example, special road tax rates as well as complete exemption from the present 'O'-licensing system.

Although the greatest percentage of showmen still operate as one-man concerns, requiring only one or two lorries and a living wagon, there are now many more larger family businesses operating adult riding machines. The heads of these families are known as 'riding masters' and have far more complex fleet requirements than the small man. For example, a modern Dodgem Track may require as many as

three lorries and two trailers. One vehicle would be equipped as a generating plant, whilst the other two lorries could be employed for carrying the base plates and nets and the dodgem cars. One trailer could carry any remaining cars, another the access steps, uprights and main structure. The pay box/amplification unit is also trailer-mounted.

The largest of all operators is the 'tenting circus', some having as many as 50 vehicles, ranging from advance publicity vans, booking offices, mobile dressing rooms and wardrobe vans to conveniences, livestock carriers, fuel and water tankers and even fire appliances.

Because of the showman's superb skill as an engineer, virtually no circus or fairground vehicle is the same as another. We have selected for publication those photographs which we feel are the most interesting or which show the most unique vehicles. The majority are arranged by chassis make, in alphabetical order.

Piet Olyslager MSIA MSAE KIVI

3A : Fred Ward's horse-drawn Galloper loads and living wagons pose on the green at Rye, Sussex, in 1918.
3B : The Rose Bros' Scammell fleet stands resplendent in their old Hounslow yard, c.1962.

THE DEVELOPMENT OF SHOWLAND TRANSPORT

Within twenty years of the appearance of Jim Myer's Bray engine, travelling showmen were becoming wise to the potential of electricity, the advantages of which were numerous. Not only did electric bulbs shed more light but the fire risk, compared with that of the arc light and its predecessor, the naphtha flare, was much reduced. The same power could also be applied to the rides, and with increased power output at his disposal the showman found it possible to introduce larger and more extravagant riding machines.

The first show engines capable of generating their own electric current appeared in 1886. An early design of Aveling & Porter featured a dynamo mounted over the big-ends. However, this layout was not generally adopted because of the large amount of oil thrown up by the motion. Instead, the dynamo was transferred to an extension at the forward end of the smokebox, an extension which eventually became an integral part of the smokebox. At first, show engines were adaptations of existing types, with the addition of smokebox extension, dynamo, etc. Being based, in the main, on the agricultural engine, these normally featured a spoked flywheel, the first show engine with a disc flywheel being Fowler No. 7036 'SUNNY BOY', supplied to Walter Marshall in 1893.

4A : The positioning of Dragon Scenic cars was a tricky problem, partly solved by the introduction of the scenic engine with its rear jib. This was Michael A. Collins's Foster 'CLAUS' at Platt Fields, Manchester, in 1945.
4B : Pat Collins's 'No.1', Burrell No. 3865, was a superb example of the Burrell scenic. Now preserved, its last showland task was to haul the Big Dipper loads from Birmingham's Crystal Palace Amusement Park to a permanent site at London's Battersea Park in 1952.
4C : E. Holland's Foden 'PRIDE OF CHESHIRE' No. 388, an early product of the Company's Sandbach works. The centre truck, three loads and two living wagons formed a typical load for this class of road loco.
4D : Tommy Essam's 'overtype' Foden (so called because the engine was located over the boiler) was rebuilt by Fodens for fairground use. The diagonally-straked wooden box body was typical of this period and examples could still be seen as late as the early 1970s, albeit on more modern diesel chassis.

4C Foden

4A Foster

4B Burrell

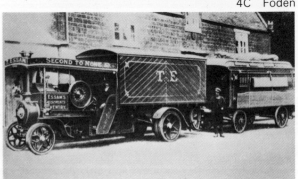
4D Foden

THE DEVELOPMENT OF SHOWLAND TRANSPORT

The familiar overall canopy and twisted brasswork did not evolve until the turn of the century, when bigger and better riding machines were at last introduced for the pleasure of adult patrons. Most spectacular of these was the Dragon Scenic, which made its debut just prior to World War I, incorporating a circular switchback carrying 'cars' weighing some 30 cwt apiece. A special version of the showman's engine, known as the 'scenic', was developed for use with this ride, the majority of these scenic types being manufactured by Charles Burrell & Sons Ltd, Thetford, Norfolk. Major differences between these and standard show engines included the provision of a rear jib crane operating off the winch system, a much larger boiler and an 'exciter' (a second dynamo located between chimney and cylinders) providing the special lighting effects for which the Dragon Scenic and its variations were renowned.

One must not think that the steam wagon was omitted from the show-land scene. Messrs Fodens Ltd, for instance, abandoned show and traction engine production in 1914 in favour of their increasingly popular wagon range, a number of these being delivered new with twisted brasswork, full-length canopies and dynamos! Many other marques appeared after their useful commercial lives were complete and a number of engines also entered, and left, the business in this way. A fascinating by-product of the show engine was the traction centre which was developed as a replacement for the Gallopers' heavy cumbrous centre engine (a modified portable design) in the days before electric drive. Frederick Savage of Kings Lynn, who developed a number of ideas perpetrated by a Mr Sidney George Soame, of Marsham, Norfolk (e.g. the original steam-powered roundabout which Soame called a Steam Circus), was responsible for the design of the traction centre, the first of which was based on his own 8 nhp single-cylinder road engine of 40 tons capacity, with hornplates extended above the motion to carry the centre spinning top (or 'cheesewheel'). While on the road, smoke and fumes were ejected via the normal chimney but when operating as a centre engine these were diverted through the hollow centre shaft of the riding machine. The traction centre, although revolutionary in theory, was far from successful. Its immense power (it was originally intended for haulage work) was too much for many of the rides, resulting in damage and injury to both rides and patrons. An attempt to

5A Savage

5B Savage

5A : Savage's first traction centre engine was 'ENTERPRISE', an 8 nhp single-cylinder model. This was of smaller dimensions than later types and was designed for use with a set of three- or four-abreast Gallopers.

5B : Pat Collins's Savage traction centre No. 847 'THE WONDER' lies derelict at Sutton Coldfield in April 1933, following conversion to a showman's haulage engine.

combat this problem was patented by Charles Burrell & Sons Ltd in 1895. This specified a separate turret-mounted engine supplying power to the motion with the main engine acting as a DC generator while stationary. No examples were built and all existing traction centres were eventually converted for normal road use.

Predecessor of the modern trailer-mounted diesel generating set was the portable electric light engine. Early examples were horse-drawn and extremely heavy, comprising a portable engine similar to that used for threshing, with dynamo mounted on a smokebox extension. Messrs Ransomes, Sims & Head (now Ransomes, Sims & Jefferies) were pioneers in this respect. Later types consisted merely of a boiler contained within a box body mounted on a trailer chassis, the dynamo being located at the forward end of the trailer. Messrs Foster of Lincoln and Thomas Green & Sons were both large-scale manufacturers of the latter.

The Steam Yachts (twin swingboats) were worked off a stationary engine, positioned between the boats, providing the motion via a chain-drive system. In the case of the smaller steam swings, this was operated by the patrons (by pulling on a rope). The much larger Steam Yachts were operator-controlled and a most impressive sight.

Although a few caterers, principally circus proprietors, were using horse transport as late as the Thirties, others had been proud owners of

6A   Ransomes, Sims & Head

6A: 6 nhp portable electric light engine No. 3895 was supplied by Messrs Ransomes, Sims & Head to the Indian Electric Light Company in 1879. Numerous machines of this type were also delivered to showmen.

6B: Anderton & Rowland's engines, named 'EARL BEATTY', 'LION', 'DRAGON', 'QUEEN MARY' and 'PRINCESS MARY', generating at Plymouth.

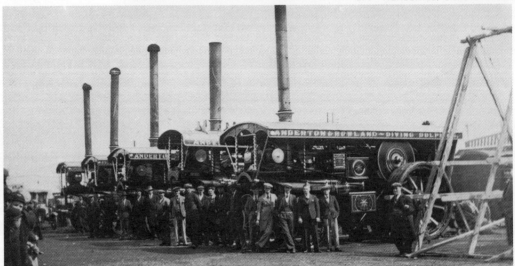

6B   Scenic engines at work

THE DEVELOPMENT OF SHOWLAND TRANSPORT

the motorcar since the early 1900s and were quick to take advantage of the internal combustion engine. Where a lot of power was required, steam was to remain in the 'front line' right up to World War II. For 'side stuff' and 'round stall' lighting purposes, however, the small petrol engine was ideal and it was not unknown for the more enterprising gentlemen to adapt their private 'runabouts' to generate when required. After World War I the 'petrol revolution' really took a hold. Vast quantities of ex-Services trucks, and other vehicles used during the hostilities, were reconditioned (many by the original manufacturers) and offered on the civilian market, principally in continental Europe and the British Isles. Low prices and, in some cases, all-wheel drive made these machines an extremely attractive proposition for the travelling showman who, being an astute businessman, was quick to snap up a bargain.

The development of the diesel engine did not have any immediate large-scale effect upon the travelling entertainment world. Caterers, in the main, continued to regard petrol and steam propulsion as their salvation and in the early days of diesel there was little in its favour to detract them from this view.

Despite this, a number of British steam vehicle manufacturers experimented with the diesel engine, some (e.g. Fowler and Yorkshire) attempting to attract custom from showland. Most projects of this nature failed. Apart from one or two exceptions (e.g. Scammell and

7A   Meadows diesel power plant

7B   Burrell

7A: Contrasting with the cumbersome portable electric light engine opposite is Armroyd Lane's diesel power plant of 1972 supplying power to his Coronation Speedway Ark. Power is supplied by a Meadows industrial unit.

7B: It was not unknown for show engines to be involved in traffic accidents, especially when running fully laden. These youngsters seem more interested in the photographer than in the plight of W. G. Danter's Burrell and loads.

Foden), the days of new show vehicles were definitely numbered, forced out by the ready availability of cheap secondhand equipment. The Fifties saw the last of the steam show engines withdrawn from service, replaced by World War II ex-Services trucks and tractors. These rugged types were the answer to the showman's prayer as steam propulsion had been virtually legislated off the road during the 1930s and it was only 'by the skin of their teeth' that some of the old engines had kept going. The advantages of all-wheel drive, short wheelbase and the ability to haul three trailers with ease were not to be sneered at!

Recent years have seen a steady increase in the use of more modern transport. Government legislation in various countries (particularly in the

8A : Even the combined tenting shows of Messrs Ringling Bros and Barnum & Bailey employed horse traction well into the Thirties. A view of this vast show in New York in 1931 shows no motor traffic in evidence.

8B : Representative of numerous ex-Services petrol-engined models which entered showland service in the Twenties was this American-built FWD Model 'B' owned by Kettering, Northants, showman Mr Harry Wright.

8C : The American Mack AC 'Bulldog' was another World War I development, many also being built for the post-war civilian market. It was a popular choice of many US showmen such as Colonel Tim McCoy who owned these attractively finished examples.

8D : The unorthodox lines of Fowler tractor No. 20892 'JUBILEE' were typical of steam manufacturers' attempts to produce a diesel-powered successor to the showman's steam road locomotive. Operated by the Nottingham concern of Hibble & Mellors Ltd, 'JUBILEE' was specially equipped for generating by Messrs Saunders.

8A Horse traction

8B FWD

8C Mack

8D Fowler

THE DEVELOPMENT OF SHOWLAND TRANSPORT

UK) has made it necessary for the travelling showman to invest in more reliable and faster vehicles—not a bad situation but one which can result in greater financial outlay than before.

Wagon construction has evolved into an exact science over the years, closely related to the constructional procedures adopted for individual rides. Riding machine components are numbered and stowed in sequence, requiring wagons and compartments of precise dimensions. It is not uncommon, therefore, for bodies to be transferred from chassis to chassis as each reaches the end of its natural life and for the same transport to accompany a particular ride when sold to a different owner. Many of the vehicles shown in this book are based on ex-military truck and tractor chassis. For illustrations of these vehicles in their original form, and further details, the reader is referred to *The Observer's Fighting Vehicles Directory—World War II* and *The Observer's Military Vehicles Directory—from 1945.*

9A: Amongst the many all-wheel drive ex-Services models snapped up by British showmen after World War II was the ex-RAF Crossley 'Q'. This version, with twin-deck frame body, was photographed at Wokingham, Berks, in 1949.

9B: Another 'de-mob' was this Austin K6 tandem-drive six-wheeler of Billy Smart's Circus, seen here at Southport in September, 1956.

9C: The striking appearance of the Michelotti-styled Scammell 'Routeman II' 8-wheeler lends itself to the attractive brushwork of the showland decorator. Both machines are owned by Messrs Rose's Pleasure Parks Ltd, of Chertsey, Surrey.

9A   Crossley

9B   Austin

9C   Scammell

AEC

10A : A popular choice with British caterers was the normal control AEC 'Mercury' of the 1930s. This example doubled as a load-carrier and living van when seen at Hampstead Heath *c.*1951.

10B : Because of their low loading qualities and easy conversion for counter sales, former passenger models were especially suitable for use as mobile snack bars, fish and chip saloons, etc. The brilliantly illuminated sign on this 1933-registered AEC 'Regal' was a sure way of attracting custom, even from the opposite side of the 'tober', site where fair is held.

10C : The AEC 'Q'-Type passenger model was unique when introduced in 1932, having an engine located on the right-hand side behind the front axle and therefore a 'fully-fronted' appearance. RG 5623 was even more unusual in that it was delivered new to Aberdeen with a rear-entrance Walker bus body instead of a front-entrance type for which this chassis was designed. It was one of only a handful of 'Q'-Types that ended their days on the fairground, in this instance as a kitchen van.

10D : Delivered new to Messrs Allen & Hanbury's Ltd in 1936, this AEC 'Matador II' later received a shortened wheelbase and single generating set for fairground operation with George Harvey Jnr, of Hendon, London, N.W.9.

10A AEC

10B AEC

10C AEC

10D AEC

11A : Rare application for the AEC (0)853 4 × 4 'Matador' of World War II was as a circus crane truck, for lifting tenting and poles. On their return to the British Isles following a South African tour, Messrs Chipperfields introduced this example which replaced a similarly-endowed Mack 6 × 6.

11B : The Ive Bros, of Dodgems and Waltzer fame, mounted a later AEC 'Mandator' cab on their 'Matador' 4 × 4 when the original structure showed signs of rusting. The drums slung beneath the body carry tax-free fuel for generating purposes.

11C : The AEC 'Militant', a post-war military six-wheeler, is rarely found on the modern showground—being a little too rugged for many operators. Robert Bros Circus, now the largest tenting show in the UK, has at least two of these employed as heavy tractors. This 6 × 6 model also carries full recovery equipment including an oxy-acetylene cutting outfit.

11D : Before his retirement, Mel Reid's Boxing & Wrestling Show was world-famous. It was carried by an AEC 'Mammoth Major III' 8-wheeler during its last years of travelling, this forming the actual base of the highly decorated booth front.

11A   AEC

11B   AEC

11C   AEC

11D   AEC

13A   Albion

13B   Albion

13C   Albion

12 : Albion's Model 35 'overtype' lorry was in production from 1927 until 1932 and was especially popular with brewing concerns. A 1931 model was owned by Pat McKeowen, of Andover, Hants, and is seen here at Redhill, Surrey, in 1952.

13A : Based on an Albion CX7N 'oiler', this unusual hybrid incorporated a Thornycroft 'Trusty' cab with AEC grille. It was owned by a member of the Southall-based Ayers family, famous for their Helter Skelter and Supercar Skymaster attractions.

13B : Messrs Ashley Bros, of Nottingham, used this strange looking vehicle with their Gallopers ride. It comprised an Albion FT15N 6 × 6 field artillery tractor of World War II vintage, equipped with a swinging boom system for loading and unloading.

13C : Albion's CX24S saw service during World War II as a tractor for a 20-ton tank and heavy equipment transporter semi-trailer. In 1946, in common with many British showmen, Messrs Botton Bros added one of these to their fleet, fitting a smart deep-skirted body, generating equipment and a large searchlight to facilitate pull-down operations after dark.

13D : The familiar Albion 'Caledonian' 8-wheelers, supplied c.1959/60 to the order of Shell-Mex & BP Ltd with unusual Alfred Miles cabs and tank bodies, have now been sold. Some, such as these two owned by James Noyce, of Farnborough, Hants, entered showland.

13D   Albion

ARMSTRONG-SAURER

14: North of England traveller Jack C. Proctor was one of a number of showmen to turn quickly to the Armstrong-Saurer diesel in the 1930s. In this view taken at Staveley, Derbys, in June 1937, was his 4/5-ton 'Diligent', with a Swiss-built Saurer in the background.

15A: Fairground operators of the Armstrong-Saurer 'Dominant' 6-wheeler were few and far between. Tom Benson & Sons' 1934-vintage long-wheelbase model had only one driven axle which must have made this machine extremely difficult to manoeuvre in soft terrain.

15B: This short-wheelbase 'Dominant' started life hauling coal in the Bradford area, being sold after a few years to John T. North, a local showman. He used it as a heavy tractor, a task for which its ruggedness was ideally suited.

15C: After World War II an Associated Daimler Model 426 single-deck rear-entrance bus, product of a brief fusion of interests between AEC and Daimler from 1926 until 1929, travelled the Midland area with a 'coconut sheet' and other 'side stuff'. AEC's 'Reliance' passenger model was based on a re-engined version of the 426.

15D: Gardner-powered 6- and 8-wheeled Atkinsons have always been more popular than lighter types of this marque. Wm. Barker & Sons' Atkinson flat, a fairly early model, is shown at the build-up of the Rugby (Warwicks) Rag Fair in August 1961.

15A   Armstrong-Saurer

15C   Associated Daimler

15B   Armstrong-Saurer

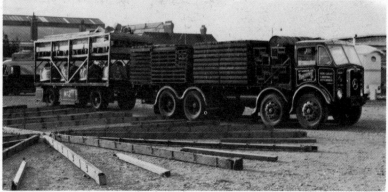

15D   Atkinson

AUSTIN, AUTOCAR

16A : One of the most spectacular and rarest of all circus acts is the human cannonball. In this case the gun, which was hydraulically actuated, was mounted on ex-WD Austin K3, employing the original searchlight mounting for which this vehicle was previously used. Many K2, K3 and K6 Austins were snapped up by showmen after the last war.

16B : The Austin K6 was a tandem-drive 3-ton 6-wheeler, of which the example shown was originally an RAF signals van. The late Billy Smart had two of these. KMO 492 is shown here at Crawley, Sussex, in the early 1960s.

16C : More recently examples of the post-war Austin military K9 4 × 4 type have appeared in civilian guise. A frequent visitor to traction engine rallies was Keith Emmett's former signals van 'FELIX'.

16D : Circo Rubi, of Madrid, were running a late-1930s American Autocar as recently as 1971. This carried tent poles, seating, etc. and featured a locally-built cab and body.

16B Austin

16C Austin

16A Austin

16D Autocar

17A   Autocar

17B   Bedford

17C   Bedford

17D   Bedford

17A : One of several Autocar U-7144T trucks operated by a fairground proprietor in Belgium. Originally it was a 4-5-ton 4 × 4 tractor truck of c.1944. It carries a generating set and has a civilian truck cab top, replacing the original canvas roof and folding windscreen.

17B : One or two examples of the OXC Bedford/Scammell tractor were acquired for showland use. Lot 563 of the March 1965 auction of Bertram Mills' transport and equipment comprised one of these units with a most unusual design of booking office semi-trailer.

17C : Fire is a constant threat to the tenting circus. To combat this, the late Billy Smart owned a succession of fire appliances, the last being a 1952 'S'-Type Bedford previously operated by the County Borough of Rochdale Fire Service. Coachwork was by Alfred Miles and equipment included a 400-gallon water tank and 500-gpm pump.

17D : Austin-based former BRS Parcels 'noddy vans' are now a common sight on every British fairground. The Bedford version, however, is extremely rare. With integral easy-access bodywork by Messrs Hawson Ltd, it was introduced at the 1968 Commercial Motor Show and is, therefore, a comparative newcomer. The example shown is believed to have been a demonstration model.

BMMO, BRISTOL, BURRELL

18A: For many years the Birmingham & Midland Motor Omnibus Company (BMMO), operating under the fleet name 'MIDLAND RED', built its own buses and coaches. Early models later travelled Midland fairgrounds in some quantity but post-war designs have not been quite so popular. This 1950-vintage S.10 underfloor-engined single-deck model was one of the exceptions.

18B: A Bristol JO5G, powered by a 5-cylinder Gardner diesel, prepares to vacate a Midland showground. This was one of a fleet of similar vehicles previously owned by United Automobile Services, Co. Durham, many of which were later acquired by showmen. These vehicles were easily identifiable by their registration letter series and 'UNITED' radiator plate.

18C: Between December 1955 and January 1964, 653 examples of the Bristol 'HA'-Series tractor model were delivered to British Road Services Ltd. Sid Squires, of Worcester, was one of many showmen to acquire this model in the early 1970s.

18D: W. Nichols' Burrell 'PRINCESS MARY' was typical of Burrell show engine production, resplendent in maroon livery and yellow wheels, the standard colour scheme adopted for their show models. Here she stands with Galloper loads at Wanstead, Essex, in 1923.

18C   Bristol

18A   BMMO

18B   Bristol

18D   Burrell

19A : In the same class as 'PRINCESS MARY' (Fig. 18D) was A. Tuby's Burrell 'THE ALDERMAN' No. 3284, looking a little the worse for wear at Balby, Lincs, in 1945.

19B : 1949 saw the withdrawal of the late William Beach's Burrell No. 3694 'LORD FISHER'. Seen here at Richmond, Surrey, in 1940, in the ownership of Miss Sally Beach, this engine was supplied new in 1915 as a 2-speed 8 nhp road locomotive and was not converted for showland use until later.

19C : One of the greatest of all British showmen was Pat Collins of Staffordshire. Burrell No. 2804 'THE GRIFFIN' is shown standing in his Bloxwich yard in 1950.

19D : Another Collins engine, No. 3391 'EMPEROR', was equipped with toothed drive to the dynamo in an attempt to prevent the drive band from slipping off the flywheel. However, this experiment was unsuccessful.

19C Burrell

19A Burrell

19B Burrell

19D Burrell

CHAMPION, CHEVROLET

20A : The unusual Champion road haulage tractor was a Perkins-engined product of Chamberlain Holdings Ltd, Welshpool, Western Australia. The only traceable example in showland was supplied to Messrs Ashton's Circus. Here it heads a road train on the Nullarbor Plain. Over terrain such as this it was claimed that the Champion could maintain 30 mph with ease!

20B : Batches of the American Chevrolet and GMC 1940/41 Dubl-Duti package delivery vans were converted into mobile canteens for use in Britain during World War II. This near original example of a 1941 Chevrolet model was spotted in the West of England some thirty years later.

20C : Chevrolet's Model 4103, a 1941 chassis with Thornton double-drive rear bogie, was a 3-ton military cargo truck ordered by the French Government but diverted to the UK. Comparison with Fig. 20B shows that the basic front end design was similar. This truck carried a 1947 civilian registration when seen at Wimbledon in 1951.

20A   Chamberlain Champion

20B   Chevrolet

20C   Chevrolet/Thornton

CHEVROLET, CITROËN, CLAYTON, COMMER

21A Chevrolet

21A: In 1952 the American Clyde Beatty Circus were using a near new COE (cab-over-engine) Chevrolet as an advance stake driver unit. It was based on a short-wheelbase tractor chassis.

21B: One of the foreign acts appearing with Chipperfields' Circus in 1962 used a Citroën coach as living accommodation. Of early Fifties vintage, body styling was typical of that period, incorporating heavy rounded contours throughout.

21C: Sam Smart, of Devizes, Wilts, mounted an early living wagon body on his secondhand Clayton wagon, seen here at Bristol in 1926. Clayton & Shuttleworth products were none too common on the fairground and although a handful of show engines were delivered few, if any, wagons were supplied new in this field.

21D: Mr George Whyatt, a foreman in the employ of Mr Charles Thurston, of Norwich, adapted this former fire brigade hose-layer for use as luxury living accommodation. It was based on an underfloor-engined Commer chassis of 1952.

21B Citroën

21C Clayton

21D Commer

CROSSLEY, DAF, DENNIS

22A Crossley

22B DAF

22C Dennis

22A: Crossley's IGL 6 × 4 3-tonner was originally used in large quantities by the RAF during World War II. It was powered by a 90-bhp 4-cylinder engine, also of Crossley manufacture, and featured Gruss air springs at the front.

22B: The Dutch Toni Boltini Circus is renowned not only for its superb programmes but also for its modern operational approach. Much of the transport fleet, for instance, is based on the home-produced DAF range, principally in 'articulated' form.

22C: Dennis Bros' 'E'-Series passenger range was announced in 1925, featuring forward-control and a 16-ft wheelbase. Like the early AECs and Bristols, the 'E' was a popular one with the showmen, frequently operating as a dual-purpose living van and load-carrier as shown here.

23A : The Dennis 'Lancet' passenger model, announced in 1933, rarely looked like this. With the exception of the one-man cab, the original body has been replaced by a box design specially adapted for the carriage of livestock. Note the small air vents high on the body sides.

23B : Mk II version of the military Dennis 'Max' 6-tonner made its debut in June 1944. Some two or three years later this example received a civilian registration, eventually entering service with a Dartford, Kent, showman.

23C : Registered in 1946, Raymond Armstrong's tandem-drive 'Jubilant', one of Dennis Bros' heavier models, clearly illustrated that advantage could be made of large flat body sides as a publicity medium.

23D : It is believed that only three eight-wheeled versions of the 'Jubilant' were completed at the Dennis Guildford works and only one is ending its days with an amusement caterer. Now owned by Eastern Counties operator Bert Stocks, this was formerly a tanker with the Eastern Gas Board.

23B Dennis

23C Dennis

23A Dennis

23D Dennis

DEUTZ, DIAMOND T

24A : Certain German caterers continue to favour the road-going industrial tractor, a design which largely disappeared in the UK with World War II. This Deutz model was observed on an *Autobahn* near Cologne in May, 1965.

24B : This heavy Diamond T tank transporter prime mover, Model 980, was taken into service by a Dutch fairground operator in 1946. Apart from the crane jib it was left in completely original condition.

24C : John Thurston, of Norwich, purchased four Diamond T 980 and 981 heavy tractors in 1946. The first of these (CCL 204) was a 981,

identifiable by the winch roller assembly in the front bumper, named 'CITY OF NORWICH'. It carried a single diesel set and travelled until quite recently with the late Mr Thurston's Dodgem Track.

24D : When Charlie Beach, a London showman, acquired Messrs Hibble & Mellors Ltd's Waltzer machine, following the latter's retirement from the business, he also purchased a Model 968 6×6 Diamond T for haulage and generating purposes, equipping this with a Leyland-powered diesel set.

24A   Deutz

24C   Diamond T

24B   Diamond T

24D   Diamond T

25A: The American Dodge VK-62B was a 3-ton chassis used in some quantities by the RAF during World War II. Several body types were fitted, including a crew coach with either integral (shown) or separate all-steel cab. This Norwich-registered example, used as a living van, was spotted at Oxford in 1952.

25B: Van conversion of an ex-US Army Dodge WC-54 field ambulance with four-wheel drive, used by a French circus in the early 1960s.

25C: The British 'D'-Series Dodge of the Sixties is not as numerous in showland as other vehicles in this class. One of the more unusual is this tractive unit of Chipperfield Bros, Amesbury, Wilts. It operates with two semi-trailers—one (shown) carrying three generating sets and the other being an extra long outfit forming the base of the Trabant (Satellite) ride.

25D: A former Dodge demonstrator was this '300'-Series 7-ton model, first registered for the 1969 season. The Luton style body was fitted by its new owner.

25A Dodge

25C Dodge

25B Dodge

25D Dodge

ERF

26A: One of few ERFs supplied new to showland before World War II was a double-drive six-wheeler in 1936. The coachbuilt integral body was particularly striking, lending itself to the traditional lettering and lining out around the cab area.

26B: Warren's shooter (shooting gallery) lorry, a 1935 ERF, was not replaced until 1970. It had been purchased second-hand from Harry Leggett, a Dorking, Surrey, haulage contractor, the Luton van body being transferred from another chassis

26B   ERF

26A   ERF

27A ERF

27D Federal

27B ERF

27C Faun

27A : Although resembling a more modern ERF, Ernest Percival & Sons' 8-wheeled Speedway truck was actually built in 1955. The cab, in fact, replaced an earlier one which had deteriorated beyond economic repair.

27B : Anyone who has attempted to reverse a lorry and trailer will understand why the modern showman prefers to shunt trailers using a front towing hitch. Using this method at his Ashford (Middx) yard, Pepper Biddall demonstrates how this should be done. The tractor, a 1961 ERF, is unique in that it was originally built to the special order of civil engineers Tilbury Maidment for the dual-purpose role of tipper or tractor.

27C : Photographed with the late Billy Smart's Circus in 1967, this Faun F 24 D props van doubled as a dressing room for its German owner. The F 24 D was a relatively light model and thus unsuitable for many showland applications.

27D : A very rare machine on British fairgrounds was the American Federal 4–5-ton 4 x 4 truck-tractor Model 94X43, used extensively by the US Armed Forces during the last war. Until 1963 one beautifully painted example was operated by William Barker & Sons (Amusements) Ltd. Note the deep-skirted body.

FODEN

28A Foden

28B Foden

28C Foden

28D Foden

28A : Foden engine No. 1540 was particularly well finished, incorporating the usual twisted brasswork and gold paint. It travelled with Simon's Bioscope Show, forerunner of the modern cinema.

28B : Earliest steamwagon owned by a British showman was J. Buller Westray's Foden, a pre-World War I model with H. C. Bauly's wooden wheels. The gentleman third from left was presumably connected with one of the proprietor's sideshows.

28C : World War I saw the end of Bauly-wheeled Fodens. Instead, 'Y'-spoked cast-steel rubber-shod wheels became standard. At about the same time the Company offered showmen such optional extras as dynamo and bracket, twisted brass, etc. Note the considerable rear overhang counterbalancing the heavier forward end.

28D : Using steamwagon parts, Fodens Ltd built 14 of these weird machines during the 1930s. Designed for timber haulage, they featured 5LW Gardner diesel engines, located in a transverse position behind the cab. This 1935 model travelled the Yorkshire area with a Mont Blanc ride soon after World War II.

29A : Axles and other running units incorporated in the 'R'- and 'S'-Type Foden diesel lorries were adapted from those used in the last of the Company's steamwagons—the 'Speed Six'. Power was supplied by a 5LW Gardner diesel.

29B : Built in 1938 to the special order of Mr W. Nichols, of Banbury, Oxon, this Model GHT6-50 was capable of hauling a gross train weight of 50 tons. Powered by a Gardner 6LW diesel, the original specification included 4-wheel hydraulic brakes and an auxiliary hand-operated worm-type cable trailer brake on the mate's side of the cab.

29C : The 'DG' cab (Fig. 29B) was replaced in 1949 by the 'FG' design, although for a year or two the 'DG' model designation continued. This 8-wheeled Luton frame with the Ferris Wheel was a DG6-15 model, a 6-cylinder engined vehicle for 15 tons gross weight.

29D : W. Nichols & Sons' 1958 'K'-Type Foden 8-wheeler is typical of many. The Hurricane Jets ride packs neatly onto this and the 'centre truck', here seen leaving a ground in June, 1972.

29B Foden

29C Foden

29A Foden

29D Foden

FORD

30A : The Fordson 'Sussex' six-wheeler was a special conversion of the Company's 30-cwt Model BB, undertaken by County Commercial Cars Ltd, of Fleet, Hants, who also marketed a single-drive version known as the 'Surrey'. This 1934 model was photographed at Reigate, Surrey, in 1951.

30B : Ford of Canada's F60S short-wheelbase 3-ton 4 × 4 of World War II rarely appeared on the fairground. This was originally a light artillery tractor but when photographed in 1967 carried a 4-cylinder Gardner lighting set.

30C : An interesting specialist machine, based in this instance on a 1951 US Ford, was the King Bros' six-wheeled canvas spool truck. Big Top canvas was wound onto two huge spools for storage and transportation between sites. Such a system is somewhat unnecessary today as canvas is supplied in easily managed lengths.

30D : Travelling with a British tenting circus in 1962 was a Dutch-registered American-built F350 Ford of 1956. The vehicle shown in the background is an Italian-registered Studebaker of 1946/47. Note the Ford's front bumper, transferred from a 1951/52 Cadillac car.

30B Ford

30C Ford

30A Fordson

30D Ford

31A: One British ex-military 3-ton 4×4 model which has found its way to UK showgrounds is this Ford Thames of the early 1950s. An unusual feature of this design was the Rootes Group cab which probably came about during pre-production experiments. It gave the vehicle the popular name of 'Commer-cab Ford'.

31B: H. Bishton's tractor 'JOHN BULL', built by William Foster & Co, of Lincoln (No. 3444), poses with loads at Derby in 1911. Note the sheeted dynamo to protect it from the ravages of dust, an all too common menace in those early days.

31C: The Rose Bros' Foster 'MAUDE' (No. 3642) has now been beautifully restored and makes occasional appearances at steam events and charity shows within easy reach of their Chertsey yard. During World War I it was used to haul wooden pit props to aid the war effort and it was at about that time that this photograph was taken, with the late Mr Jack Rose, and son Freddie, seated in front.

31A Ford

31B Foster

31C Foster

FOWLER, FWD

32B Fowler

32A Fowler

32C FWD

32D FWD

32A : Frequently in dispute is the number of wagons hauled by showman's road locomotives in their heyday. Here's the 'proof'. No fewer than eight, carrying Martin & Sons' Gondolas, were coupled behind their Fowler 'ELECTRIC' (No. 8331) when this photograph was taken at Hucknall, Notts. The date is uncertain.

32B : How the majority of show engines ended their days. Fowler No. 9456 'MARINA' was built to the special order of Mrs T. Smith, Shoreham, Sussex, in 1905.

32C : Now preserved by Mr V. Kirk, of Oxford, this British-assembled FWD Model 'B' first saw the light of day towards the end of World War I. It was converted for showland use during the Twenties and later re-engined and fitted with pneumatic tyres.

32D : In 1945 Messrs Traylen Bros, of Feltham, Middx, acquired a 1929 R6T (rigid 6-wheeled tractor) FWD. It had been produced in Britain (as FWD-England) and was powered by an AEC engine. In 1959 it was sold for scrap through lack of spares. One or two of these impressive machines have survived. During the mid-1930s they were produced by AEC. Very early models had a Dorman engine.

FWD, GARRETT, GILFORD

33A   FWD

33B   Garrett

33C   Gilford

33A: The last FWD Model SU-COE on British fairgrounds was EEW 660, Miss Sally Beach's heavy tractor 'LORD FISHER'. The nameplate came from her early Burrell (Fig. 19B). Most of these once rather common 'Sucoes', as they were called, started life as artillery tractors with the British and Canadian Armies in World War II.

33B: Garrett 8 nhp road locomotive 'EMPRESS OF JAPAN' (No. 25814) was supplied to Swales Forrest early in 1907. It was built by the Richard Garrett Engineering Works Ltd, Leiston, Lincs. Photographed in Cann Hall Road, Forest Gate, London, in 1911, the loads comprised Forrest's Razzle Dazzle (early form of Rotor). Henry Forrest, who could not drive, stands on the footplate.

33C: 1929 saw the introduction of the Gilford 168OT passenger model, powered by an American Lycoming engine of 6-litre capacity. This model, in second-hand form, was favoured by the smaller showland operators, often doubling (as here) as load-carrier and living accommodation. Like the Crossley IGL (Fig. 22A), Gruss air springs were fitted at the front.

GMC, GUY

34A : GMC's Model CCKW-353 2½-ton 6 × 6 saw a variety of applications during World War II. This version, however, received its metal-panelled body after the war. The CCKW Series was another British fairground rarity. On the Continent of Europe these vehicles appeared in fair numbers.

34B : Acquired for show use in 1946, this ancient-looking machine was a pre-World War II Guy FBAX 6-wheeler originally intended for searchlight duties. It was seen at Hendon, North London, in April 1950.

34C : Some 2000 examples of the 'Arab II' passenger model left the Guy factory between 1942 and 1947, many ending their lives in the hands of showmen. Former East Kent BJG 414 of 1945, powered by a 5LW Gardner diesel engine, received the usual fairground adaptations including removal of the roof and blocking in of certain lower saloon windows.

34D : Messrs T. Whitelegg & Sons Ltd, Plymouth, Devon, purchased two double-drive 'Invincible' truck-mixer chassis in 1970. These were completely transformed from near total wrecks, replacing two of the operator's Thornycroft 'Amazon' tractors (Fig. 55). Here, 'THE GLADIATOR' hauls the No. 1 Dodgem loads out of Lipson Vale, Plymouth, in June 1970.

34A GMC

34C Guy

34B Guy

34D Guy

HANOMAG, IKARUS

35A: The attractively styled living van body on this Hanomag road tractor chassis of the Thirties was to an old-established Continental design. This specimen was travelling in Belgium long after the War.

35B: The Hanomag SS100 was a purpose-built powerful road tractor, developed for long-distance haulage work on the new German *Autobahnen* of the 1930s. The standard design was as shown here, with coachbuilt crewcab, fuel tank and ballast at the rear.

35C: One marque almost unheard of in the British Isles but which travelled with Billy Smart's Circus during its last season was the Ikarus passenger model. This was a dual entrance/exit model with roof luggage space, built near Budapest, Hungary.

35A   Hanomag

35B   Hanomag

35C   Ikarus

INTERNATIONAL, KARRIER

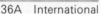
36A   International

36B   International

36C   Karrier

36D   Karrier

36A : This late 1920s International bus originally carried 18 or 20 passengers. It was typical of a period (1930–50) when many of the smaller operators acquired second-hand passenger models which could be easily adapted to serve both as load-carriers and for living accommodation. Although photographed in 1950, the left-hand headlamp still carried its wartime mask !

36B : Circus Gruss, a French tenting circus, based its 'heavy' fleet on ex-military International Model H-542-11 truck-tractors. All had extended front ends to accommodate new Berliet engines, this example having a further extension to take a power winch. In this instance, the Big Top has been set up in a French market place and the vehicle was used as an anchorage point for guy ropes. These 'Inters' were quite popular in France and the Low Countries.

36C : A 1930-registered Karrier, photographed in Henry Gray's Mitcham (Surrey) winter quarters, also typified the 1930–50 period. As in so many other cases, a traditionally-styled wooden van body with extra roof storage facilities was carried.

36D : Karrier Motors' CK3 was a post-war 3-ton forward-control model, one of their most popular for municipal applications. Miss Sally Beach ran this Luton-bodied example with her Gallopers ride.

KARRIER, KNOX-MARTIN, LAND-ROVER

37A : Not strictly a fairground or circus vehicle, this 1965 Karrier 'Bantam' was modified by Kent enthusiast George Marsh to carry an early Dutch street organ to and from steam rallies in the South of England. The box body, which he built himself, was designed to open out as shown.

37B : The American Knox-Martin 3-wheeled tractor is believed to have been the first true 'mechanical horse'. Powered by a 60-hp engine, 'BIG BROTHER' could turn in its own length and was a popular publicity attraction at the Sells Floto—Buffalo Bill Circus during World War I.

37C : The Land-Rover is a popular and useful general-purpose vehicle for fairground and circus proprietors. John Biddall, of Hampstead, London, is one of a number of operators to use the Land-Rover for publicity work. As well as advertising the fair on the road, it can be used as an advance unit for fixing posters.

37A Karrier

37B Knox-Martin

37C Land-Rover

LEYLAND

38A: The 'Titan' passenger model, introduced in 1927 as the TD1, was a much sought after series for British travellers. This TD1, delivered to Southdown with a Short Bros highbridge body, was hardly advertising tyre safety when photographed at Sutton, Surrey, in June 1956!

38B: One unique adaptation of the TD1 was Wm. Barker & Sons (Amusements) Ltd's former Crosville model. Starting life as a rear-entrance double-decker, it ended its days as a dual-purpose load-carrier, with part box and part frame body. Here it is with Dodgem loads at the 1961 Rugby Rag Fair.

38C: One cage in the Leyland 'menagerie' was occupied by the 'Bull' goods model, a robust heavy-duty 4-wheeled model snapped up by showmen on the second-hand market. Over the years Messrs E. Ashcroft & Sons, of Barnsley, have owned a whole procession of Leylands of the class. 'DILIGENT' would be worth its weight in gold if it were still around today, particularly in this condition.

38B Leyland

38A Leyland

38C Leyland

38D: Production of the 3-ton tandem-drive 'Retriever', produced for British military use during the late Thirties and World War II, topped 6500. The 'snout' on this example was made necessary by the replacement of the original 4-cylinder engine by a trusty Gardner diesel, known in the trade as 'the showman's friend'.

38D Leyland

LEYLAND

39A   Leyland

39B   Leyland

39A: The 'Hippo' Mk II was a 10-ton 6 × 4 military load carrier, introduced in 1944. The low body silhouette of J. T. Herbert's 'Hippo' frame, seen here with Dodgem loads at Shaftesbury, Dorset, in June 1969, resulted in an attractively proportioned truck. A generating set was located immediately to the rear of the cab.

39B: Amongst the most popular of all 'heavy' fairground Leylands was the post-war 'Octopus', entire fleets of which were acquired by caterers during the Fifties and Sixties. This former London Brick Company model was spotted pulling into Oxford St. Giles in September 1970. Note the individual dust covers for each of the Dodgem cars.

39C: At Christmas there are one or two fairs held in certain parts of the British Isles. Some showmen find these a little awkward, being in the middle of the 'off' season with vehicles de-licensed and rides and equipment undergoing repairs and re-decoration. It is also a time, however, when much of the 'new' transport for the coming season makes its debut, such as this later version of the 'Octopus' at Rochdale, Lancs. This was purchased only a few days previously and still carried its previous owner's name and address.

39C   Leyland

40 : An example of the 18-ton Mack EXBX 6 × 4 tank transportation unit, part of a cancelled French Government contract diverted to Britain early in World War II, entered showland with Messrs J. T. Herbert, of Dorchester, Dorset, in 1947. The original two-man cab was rebuilt to a larger size but the original doors were re-used. The wheelbase was shortened considerably. Similar tank carriers which entered showland after 'demob' were the White-Ruxtalls shown on pages 58/59.

41A : HKD 5, one of two Model NM6 6 × 6 Macks owned by Lancashire riding master H. J. Wallis (the other was HKD 6), travelled with a Waltzer ride. 'NM'-Series Macks of World War II were probably the most popular of this marque in the British Isles, especially with showmen and, at the other extreme, for show-clearing purposes.

41B : An interesting feature of the 'NM'-Series Mack was its ability to deal with the stickiest ground, by combining 6 × 6 capabilities with dual tyre equipment *all round*! In practice, however, dual tyres on the front axle were rarely required as it was unusual for these machines to be beaten by ground conditions.

41C : Henry Botton's 'NM' was typical of heavy generating outfits owned by British riding masters. No space was wasted and the twin Gardner-powered sets were enclosed within a box-style body incorporating drop canopies, etc.

41D : The 'NM's big sister was the 7½-ton 'NO'-Series, the 'NM' being a 6-tonner. Travelling at speed between grounds is R. Townsend & Sons' (Weymouth, Dorset) NO2 'THE LEADER' with Noah's Ark loads. Just visible at the rear of the tractor is a special davit, modern counter-part of the rear-mounted crane equipment specified for scenic engines. Commonly known as 'Super Mack', the 'NO'-Series trucks are also popular for conversion to recovery vehicles.

41B   Mack

41C   Mack

41A   Mack

41D   Mack

MAUDSLAY

42A: The postwar Maudslay 'Mogul' was another popular choice in the medium-weight range. This 1947 model travelled for many years with an Oxfordshire showman, who used it both as a load-carrier and as a kitchen van.

42B: The Appleton family, famous for their parading shows and similar attractions, ran a Maudslay 'Mustang' twin-steer 6-wheeled van as recently as 1972. Following its absorption into the ACV Group, the 'Mustang' name was transferred to the AEC factory at Southall, which produced a considerable number of twin-steer models bearing this name during the Fifties and Sixties.

42C: Maudslay's 6-wheeler was known as the 'Maharajah'. 'DREAD-NOUGHT' was scrapped in 1968, the body being transferred to Atkinson L. 1066 twin-steer 6-wheeler 329 FRE.

42A   Maudslay

42B   Maudslay

42C   Maudslay

43A: The last showland operators of the famous Maudslay 'Meritor' 8-wheeler were W. Nichols, of Banbury, Oxon, and Frank Wilson, of Redditch, Worcs, the former with the Dodgems and the latter the Waltzer. Nichols' version, here seen entering Oxford St. Giles, was ousted by the Leyland shown in Fig. 39B.

43B: J. & H. McLaren Ltd, of Leeds, sold most of their steam show engines to North of England travellers. No. 1623 'GOLIATH' was a 10 nhp model supplied to Pat Collins, of Bloxwich. Show engines of the McLaren works were easily identifiable by the angular smoke-box extension carrying the dynamo.

43C: In common with Fowler's attempts to manufacture a successful diesel-propelled machine, the McLaren works supplied a unique design to Messrs Pickfords towards the end of the 1930s. Unlike the Fowler design, this vehicle was of forward-control layout but retained the traction type 'hind wheels'. In 1952 it passed to Yorkshire showman W. H. Church for use with his Noah's Ark.

43B   McLaren

43A   Maudslay

43C   McLaren

44A   Mercedes-Benz

44B   Mercedes-Benz

44C   Morris-Commercial

44A : Apart from enthusiasm for the Mercedes marque on British grounds during the Thirties and Forties, products of this German manufacturer have appeared in relatively small quantities. On the Continent, of course, they were more common, as exemplified here by circus artiste Willy Lenz's van of the 1950s. The caravan is of special interest, having Ackermann steering.

44B : A more modern Mercedes-Benz, with stepframe horsebox semi-trailer, is one of a fleet used by the Dutch Circus Toni Boltini. The portion of the body above the semi-trailer 'fifth wheel' is given over to employees' accommodation and the whole used as stable area while on site.

44C : This weird machine, based on a Morris-Commercial 4 x 4 chassis of World War II, travelled with Chipperfields' Circus from 1959. The vehicle was driven into the arena where a young girl climbed into the tank with two alligators as companions !

44D : Top of the popularity poll for many of the smaller British operators was the 5-ton BMC van. Now superseded by the functionally-designed 'noddy van', the 'FF' and 'FH'-Series BMC (Austin and Morris) were frequently acquired by showmen as soon as they appeared on the second-hand market. This Morris is travelled by a member of the Middlesex-based Searle family.

44D   Morris

45A: Motor Traction Ltd established their manufacturing concern near Croydon, Surrey, in 1951 and were in business for precisely seven years. Claimed to be the last MTN Rutland in regular service, the vehicle shown was owned by Miss Sally Beach until its replacement by a Karrier (see Fig. 36D).

45B: By using similar body panels, this mid-1950s German Opel 'Blitz' kitchen van bore a striking resemblance to its contemporary, the British Bedford, both being products of the General Motors Corporation and, in turn, patterned on Chevrolet's 1947 truck styling. Coachwork was typical of Continental European design, incorporating rubber and alloy rubbing strips. Note the British registration.

45C: Another British marque popular at one time was the Pagefield, manufactured by the Pagefield Iron Works, Wigan, Lancs, from 1907 to 1951. After that date production was continued by Walker Bros (Wigan) Ltd. Many of the pre-war designs were attractive for their day, such as this 1936 model with deep-skirted body seen at Reigate, Surrey, in 1951.

45B   Opel

45A   MTN Rutland

45C   Pagefield

RANSOMES

JOHN COTTRELL'S GALLOPING PIGS.

REO, SAVA-AUSTIN, SAVAGE

46: Ransomes, Sims & Jefferies 8 nhp compound show engine No. 20217 'SURPRISE' was supplied new to Mr John Cottrell in May, 1908. This was typical of the few show engines built by this Ipswich, Suffolk, engineering concern.

47A: In 1950 Reo built the first US Army Ordnance 'M-Series' 2½-ton 6×6 trucks, popularly referred to as 'Eager Beavers'. The only British-operated show trucks of this type were owned by the late Billy Smart, each being equipped as a standby generating unit. 897 AMO normally hauled the Nos. 1 and 2 Booking Office trailers between sites. Note spare wheel below the original front-mounted winch.

47B: Using BMC parts, the Spanish firm of Soc. Anon. Vehiculos Automoviles assembles commercials under the Sava-Austin name. This 'FG' Model with Robert Bros Circus for 1972 started life as a minicoach. The Sava-Austin is relatively common in Spain but confined exclusively to circus artistes in the UK.

47C: Savage traction centre No. 730 'EMPRESS' was delivered to Barker, Thurston & Sons, Norwich, in 1898. She was Savage's first double-crank compound engine, of 8 nhp, with full-length canopy and a small steam organ in place of the dynamo.

47A Reo

47B Sava-Austin

47C Savage

SCAMMELL

48A Scammell

48B Scammell

48C Scammell

48D Scammell

48A: The Scammell, of course, requires no introduction. Supplied c.1930 to the special order of Messrs Jacob Studt Jnr & Sons, this chain-driven model is claimed to have been the first Scammell delivered new to a showman. The dynamo was by Messrs Maudsley, of Dursley, Glos. The vehicle was scrapped in 1966.

48B: One of the first Scammell generating tractors supplied new ex-works with an 'integral' body was a chain-driven model for operation with John W. Hoadley's Moon Rocket ride during the early Thirties. This machine may still exist as it continued to operate well into the Sixties.

48C: Isle of Wight travellers, the Arnold Bros, were well known throughout the island and on the adjacent mainland. Heading a typical road-train of the period, this generating outfit of 1932 was specially converted for show use by G. Baker & Sons, Southampton, a fairground family now involved in road haulage of abnormal loads.

48D: Most popular of all wartime Scammells was the 6 × 4 'Pioneer' type, supplied in various forms. A small fleet of Model R100 heavy artillery tractors was used by Dorking, Surrey, caterers Tom Benson & Sons for a number of years. The example shown here was one of the first, being acquired in 1950.

49A: An immaculately turned out example of the SV/2S 'Pioneer' recovery tractor was travelled by Bernard Cole & Sons, Southampton, for many years. The integral body incorporated a roller shutter at the rear. Later, 'SIR HILARY' as it was called (to commemorate the 1953 Everest Expedition) passed to Jimmy Williams, of Tadley, Hants, and finally into preservation with Steve and Vicky Postlethwaite, of Salisbury, Wilts.

49B: Scammell's first 4 × 4 model, a prototype gun tractor for the Admiralty, was delivered in March 1939. After the war it passed to Messrs Rose Bros, of Hounslow, Middx, now trading as Rose's Pleasure Parks Ltd. It was completely rebuilt by Reall Coachbuilders Ltd, Slough, Bucks, the Scammell petrol engine being replaced by a 6LW Gardner 'oiler', other alterations including a coachbuilt cab and body and a rear jib crane for lifting the Skid centre. In 1970 the bicycle-type front wings (or 'cycle wings') were replaced by box-type units as shown and the whole given a repaint. (See also Fig. 3B).

49C: The 4 × 4 was so successful that John and Freddie Rose purchased its successor, a 'Mountaineer' drawbar tractor previously owned by Wrekin Roadways Ltd, Wellington, Salop. It did not live up to expectations, however, and was resold within a year to Henry Anderson for operation with his Dive Bomber ride. This early view with Rose's Pleasure Parks shows the high body mounting and stand-by lighting set added by the Rose brothers.

49A Scammell

49B Scammell

49C Scammell

SCAMMELL

HY STUDTS & SONS

HENRY STUDTS & SONS

AMUSEMENT PROVIDERS

SWANSEA

HSS

"HIS MAJESTY"

SCAMMELL

DWN 766

50 : The only diesel-engined machine delivered new to showmen in any quantity was the Scammell/Harrison 'Showtrac', based on a new 20-ton chassis which made its debut in 1946. First production model was delivered to Henry Studts & Sons, Swansea. This had no winch or dynamo—just a wooden ballast box body. It was named 'HIS MAJESTY'.

51A : The more common integral-bodied 'Showtrac' carried a 450-Amp Maudsley dynamo bolted to the heavy ballast block. The controls for the power winch were on the mate's side of the cab and the dynamo driven off a power take-off via five heavy-gauge rubber belts. Bodywork by Messrs Brown Bros, of Tottenham, was added later and the vehicle returned to the Watford plant for painting and lettering.

51B : Although this vehicle appears to be identical to the official demonstration model (see Fig. 52) it was, in fact, a conversion based on a tractor chassis first registered in June 1937. The Swindon-based Edwards concern had two such conversions, both of which were undertaken by Sidney Harrison Ltd, official 'Showtrac' distributors.

51C : On this Scammell 'Showtrac', registered in Doncaster in 1946, the dynamo was driven by a chain from a PTO-driven sprocket on the side of the chassis. Vehicle is shown before completion of the bodywork.

51D : Bird's eye view of a 'Showtrac' on the production line at Scammell's Watford works.

51A Scammell

51B Scammell

51C Scammell

51D Scammell

The *Scammell* SHOWTRAC

52 : The only 'Showtrac' demonstrator was finished in the livery of Sidney Harrison Ltd of Bury St. Edmunds in Suffolk, the official distributors. Mr Harrison had formerly been a salesman of Burrell show tackle. The demonstrator made its public debut at the 1946 Oxford St. Giles Fair, with Mr John Thurston, who did not, however, purchase any. The vehicle featured : 100-bhp diesel engine, 450-Amp dynamo, fully-equipped switchboard, four-wheel air-operated brakes with connection for trailers, 'Easy Fit' tracks for rear wheels, coachbuilt bodywork, power winch and six-speed constant-mesh gearbox. The weight, fully equipped, was quoted as $9\frac{3}{4}$ tons.

53A : Powered by a 108-bhp Perkins R6 diesel engine, the normal-control version of the Mk 12 Seddon was never a common sight, even in commercial circles. Engine access was excellent with wide worktop surfaces on the front wings.

53B : The underfloor-engined Sentinel of post-war years is another machine which has appeared in showland only occasionally. The 6-wheeled model, designated Types 4/6DV or 6/6DV depending upon whether a 4- or 6-cylinder engine was fitted, was not as common in showland as the 4-wheeler. F. Thompson, of Lincoln, was still running one as recently as 1972.

53C : The SOS passenger model was announced in 1923, based on a design developed by a Mr Shire, who was at that time Chief Engineer of the Birmingham & Midland Motor Omnibus Co (otherwise known as 'Midland Red'). One batch of SOS 'DON' models, delivered in 1935, received forward-entrance bodies by Short Bros and Brush. One of these, former Midland Red No. 1711, carried a small generating set for lighting 'side stuff' and round stalls.

53D : Supplied new to caterer Mr T. Frankham, of Bristol, in 1918, Tasker 'Little Giant' No. 1778 'MARSHAL FOCH', a product of Messrs Wm. Tasker & Sons Ltd, later passed to Anderton & Rowlands Ltd, of Bristol and Plymouth. Originally, it had been equipped with diagonally-straked steel-shod rear wheels.

53C SOS

53A Seddon

53B Sentinel

53D Tasker

THORNYCROFT

54A   Thornycroft

54B   Thornycroft

54C   Thornycroft

54D   Thornycroft

54A: Complete with wartime headlamp masks, this elderly van-bodied Thornycroft was still in regular use during the early Fifties, travelling with a 'coconut sheet'.

54B: Thornycroft's 'Stag' was a single-drive 6-wheeler (6 × 2), announced in 1935. London & Home Counties traveller Henry Cheeseman converted his into a 4-wheeler, seen here at Hampstead in 1951.

54C: Identifiable only by its distinctive rear hubs, Henry Gray's Bristol-radiatored Thornycroft 'Tartar' 3-ton 6 × 4 WOF model was one of many disposed of by the military after the last war. A PTO-driven dynamo and completely new cab were fitted by Mr Gray.

54D: An example of the first design of 8-wheeled Thornycroft 'Trusty' travelled for a number of years with Birmingham showman Mr Harry Ayers. This carried a Cake Walk machine which, when built up, used the lorry as its base and power supply. In recent years the Cake Walk has enjoyed a new lease of life at the increasingly popular old time fairs.

55: Three Thornycroft 'Amazon' short-wheelbase 6 × 4 models, supplied new to West of England caterers T. Whitelegg & Sons Ltd just after the Second World War were reportedly part of a cancelled military order. 'THE GLADIATOR', seen here with partially completed bodywork, remained in service until 1970.

TILLING-STEVENS

56A Tilling-Stevens

56A: George Pickard's 1914 petrol-electric model started life as a Brighton Corporation bus, passing to Mr Pickard in 1926. It was converted to pneumatic tyres during the Thirties and now makes regular appearances at old time fairs and steam rallies.

56B: Unlike Pickard's Tilling (Fig. 56A), Frank Sedgewick's petrol-electric retained its original rear-entrance single-deck body. This was believed to have been supplied new to the Trent Motor Omnibus Co and was still travelling when photographed in 1968.

56C: The Tilling-Stevens 'Express' bus was first shown at the 1925 Commercial Motor Show. For a time, second-hand models were especially popular on the fairground but, as spares began to get short after the last war, so the few remaining examples were withdrawn. This former East Surrey model was spotted in 1951.

56B Tilling-Stevens

56C Tilling-Stevens

57A : A considerable number of searchlight trucks based on Tilling chassis was produced just prior to World War II. Nearly 200 such units, utilizing the Company's TS19/8 4-ton model, were supplied to the War Office from 1936 to 1938. These were to be a popular choice for showmen in later years because of their excellent generating capabilities.

57B : In 1939 and 1940 the Company supplied their TS20 3-ton model specially adapted for searchlight work. Power was produced by a 70-bhp 4-cylinder Tilling 5V petrol engine located within the cab. Ahead of this lay the dynamo providing current to the searchlight equipment, hence the 'snout' nose effect.

57C : The Vulcan 6PF, also built by Tilling-Stevens Motors Ltd, Maidstone, Kent, was offered in long- and short-wheelbase forms, featuring a smart coachbuilt cab with detachable nearside front wing facilitating engine access. This Luton-type van travelled on the R. Edwards (Swindon) circuit.

57B Tilling-Stevens

57A Tilling-Stevens

57C Vulcan

58: The most famous fairground Whites in the UK are undoubtedly the pair owned by Southampton showman Mr Bernard Cole. Both are Model 922 White-Ruxtalls, originally employed as tank carriers by the British armed forces during the North African campaign. For showland use, the wheelbase was shortened and the bonnet extended some 12 in to accommodate a Gardner 6LW power unit. A short sub-frame with drawbar equipment was added at the front. The unit on the left (GEL 614) was named 'MASTERPIECE' and carried one generating set in an attractively pannelled rear body. The one on the right (KEL 500) was christened 'MORNING STAR' and was fitted with two generating sets.

59A: Another view of Mr Cole's fine brace of Whites, like Fig. 58 taken by Mr R. M. Collis at Pennington Common in June, 1970. Note the spotlight on the cab of 'MORNING STAR' (at one time fitted on both).

59B: 'MORNING STAR' with Waltzer loads at Christchurch Quay, Hampshire, in August, 1969.

59C: Also travelling in the Home Counties at that time were Messrs Brett Bros, again with a Waltzer machine. For this they used a White Model 666, also powered by a Gardner 6LW. Basically the White 666 was similar in design to the Mack 'NM'-Series (q.v.).

59D: The Spanish Circo Rubi (see also Fig. 16D) continued to use a somewhat dilapidated 1936 Russian ZIS-5 3-tonner during their 1971 season. There are still a number of Russian commercials of this period in Spain today. These were imported during the Civil War of 1936.

59B White

59C White

59D ZIS

59A White

MISCELLANEOUS WAGONS AND TRAILERS

At the turn of the century the travelling showman's living accommodation consisted mainly of horse-drawn 'romany' type vans. As steam traction gained an ever increasing hold, larger and heavier vans became possible and in this way a style was developed which is now traditionally associated with the travelling amusement caterer.

Based on 4-wheeled trailer chassis of varying dimensions, these wagons are as popular now as they ever were, frequently changing hands at quite high prices. Some designs by Messrs Orton, Sons & Spooner cost as much as £3000 new in the Thirties. A 30 ft wagon weighing some ten tons, for instance, was delivered to Wm. Murphy at that time. Featuring electric heat and light, it cost between £3000 and £4000. Now more modern designs can also be found, the current trend being towards semi-trailer types.

60B   Canvas Spool Wagon

60A   Band Wagon

60C   Living Wagon

60D   Living Wagon

60A : Horse-drawn circus bandwagons of the type used in the USA were among the most ornate of all show vehicles. The beautifully carved woodwork was invariably finished in gold and even the seating for the band was an integral part of the wagon.

60B : The canvas spool wagon, designed to simplify the handling of Big Top canvas, appeared as early as the turn of the century. This horse-drawn wagon of the Sells Floto Circus was one of the earliest.

60C : Messrs Orton, Sons & Spooner designed and built living wagons of all types, frequently to the customers' individual requirements. Typical was this 28 ft model delivered about 1936. The bay window, clerestory roof and underboxes were normal showland features.

60D : Occasionally, one comes across more modern custom-built designs embodying many of the features incorporated in earlier designs. This highly customized streamlined design was mounted on a 4-wheeled lengthened trailer chassis, again incorporating a clerestory-style roof.

MISCELLANEOUS WAGONS AND TRAILERS

Weight was one of the greatest problems for the early showman. A case in point was Bostock & Wombwell's elephant wagon which measured 30 ft long × 9 ft wide, grossing eight tons plus payload. Each of the six wheels, furthermore, was 18 in in width and 30 horses were necessary on an upgrade. Weak bridges had to be propped with timber baulks before this wagon could pass, and road and bridge tolls were exorbitant.

Today, good use is made of full-trailers (independent drawbar types) for load-carrying. In the UK up to three trailers can be hauled by a single tractor at any one time, provided that the overall length is no more than 7 metres, the three together making up a complete riding machine. Of these, one may well be a 'centre truck', with two or four wheels. Originally, this would have comprised a solid-tyred unit, complete with steam engine to provide power, cruciform hub, centre drum and mechanism. Later types, from c.1930, were mounted on pneumatic tyres and normally equipped for electric drive. Once again, Frederick Savage was a pioneer in this respect. His 3-abreast Gallopers were packed into just three loads—two wagons and a 'centre truck' plus organ. This was easily handled by one traction engine at a gross train weight (excluding engine) of approximately 37 tons.

61A 'Centre Truck'

61A : Wm. Bagnall, a Staffordshire showman, was still using a solid-tyred 'centre truck' for his 3-abreast Gallopers in 1958. Although the steam centre engine remained intact, the ride was actually driven by an electric motor mounted alongside. Towing lorry was a World War II 6 × 4 Model BY5 Albion.

61B : Former Services anti-aircraft and searchlight trailers now form the basis for most 'centre trucks', being designed for jacking level on a firm base.

61B 'Centre Truck'

Other types are too numerous to detail in full. Principally, there are packing, box and frame trailers, mobile generating plants, king-pole trailers and animal cages. Semi-trailers are now becoming more common in many countries, especially in the USA where state regulations do not normally allow road-trains of the type prevalent in European countries.

62A: John Thurston's scenic scenery van (the leading wagon shown here) was designed and built by Messrs Orton, Sons & Spooner. It was intended for rail travel, being built to railway loading gauge and equipped with only small wheels to ease movement between site and railhead. This was a posed publicity shot in Wisbech Market Place, using an International industrial tractor supplied by local dealer Bodger Bros Ltd.

62B: Box trucks and cage vans used by Chipperfields Circus during the 1950s carried superb examples of showland painting and lettering, exemplified by this animal cage.

62C: The Willy Hagenbeck Circus on the Continent of Europe uses a variety of animal wagons. One is based on a Continental living wagon style, complete with clerestory roof, chimney and shutters for the windows!

62D: Transport of John Beach & Sons, Ashford, Middx, is amongst the most attractively finished in the UK. This open-topped box wagon, travelling with the Gallopers, is typical. Note the dual wheels all round.

62B   Animal Cage Van

62C   Animal Cage Van

62D   Box Van

62A   Scenery Van

MISCELLANEOUS WAGONS AND TRAILERS

63A: The requirements of a modern tenting circus are totally dissimilar to those of the travelling showman. Special vehicles have to be developed to handle the king-poles for example. Here, a six-wheeled drawbar wagon has been specially adapted to transport some of the smaller poles used by the Billy Smart combine during its final travelling season.

63B: Another six-wheeled circus wagon, with dual tyres all round, is used by the Robert Bros Circus to transport its elephants. This is an ex-Services wagon built to special order by R. A. Dyson, of Liverpool.

63C: Chance Mfg. Co Inc, of Wichita, Kansas, are specialists in the design and construction of juvenile and adult riding machines. The Trabant (known in the UK as the Satellite) is mounted as standard on a tandem-axle semi-trailer outfit, requiring no other transport. Using the semi-trailer as a base, the ride can be ready to open inside three hours. This machine is also built under licence by Ivan Bennett Engineering in the British Isles.

63A   Pole Wagon

63B   Elephant Wagon

63C   Riding Machine Base Semi-Trailer

INDEX

ACKNOWLEDGEMENTS

This book was compiled and written largely from historical source material in the library of the Olyslager Organisation, and in addition photographs and/or other material was kindly provided or loaned by several collectors/enthusiasts, notably Messrs N. J. R. Baldwin, Colin J. Ball, S. J. Beaton, D. H. Busley, R. M. Collis, F. B. Comely, B. J. Edwards, A. Gagen, A. Imber, David Jamieson, Alan W. Jenkins, R. Jolly, A. S. Jones, Robert F. Mack, T. J. Mason, the late Jack Mellor, M. R. M. New, C. B. Parcell, Alan Pepper, John Ray, J. H. Reohorn, J. R. Scott, F. Sedgwick, H. J. Visor, Jack Wilkinson ('Cyclist'), A. G. Wilson and P. L. Wright.
Thanks are also extended to Circus World Museum (Baraboo, Wisc., USA), CVRTC Photos, DNM Automotive, the Fairground Society Hazlestrine Photos, JD Transport Photographs, and the University of Reading, for the use of illustrations.